HORRIBLE SCIENCE

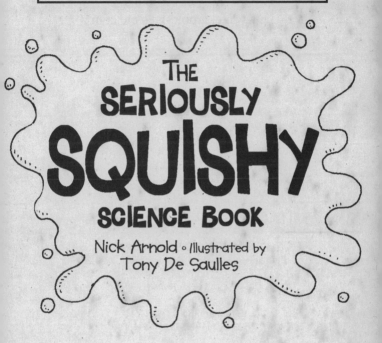

THE
SERIOUSLY
SQUISHY
SCIENCE BOOK

Nick Arnold ∘ Illustrated by
Tony De Saulles

D0552953

■SCHOLASTIC

Visit Nick Arnold at
www.nickarnold-website.com

Scholastic Children's Books,
Euston House, 24 Eversholt Street,
London NW1 1DB, UK

A division of Scholastic Ltd
London ~ New York ~ Toronto ~ Sydney ~ Auckland
Mexico City ~ New Delhi ~ Hong Kong

First published in the UK by Scholastic Ltd, 2007

10 digit ISBN 0 439 94414 7
13 digit ISBN 978 0439 94414 4

Printed and bound by GGP Media GmbH, Poessneck, Germany

2 4 6 8 10 9 7 5 3 1

CONTENTS

Nick Arnold has been writing stories and books since he was a youngster, but never dreamt he'd find fame writing about Squishy Science. His research included reading Horrible Science books and wondering where he found all those foul facts, and he enjoyed every minute of it.

When he's not delving into Horrible Science, he spends his spare time eating pizza, riding his bike and thinking up corny jokes (though not all at the same time).

Tony De Saulles picked up his crayons when he was still in nappies and has been doodling ever since. He takes Horrible Science very seriously and even agreed to try out the make-your-own zombie kit. Fortunately, he has made a full recovery.

When he's not out with his sketchpad, Tony likes to write poetry and play squash, though he hasn't written any poetry about squash yet.

INTRODUCTION

Most people think that science is serious. Seriously dreary, seriously brain-dead and seriously boring. They imagine that science is all about brainy boffins doing strange things to test tubes and long, l-o-n-g lessons in smelly school labs…

But most people are wrong. Science isn't boring – it's horrible! And when Science is horrible it comes to life in an exciting way.

We've taken the most seriously horrible bits of Horrible Science and squished them into the pages of this book (and a very messy job it was too). So read on, brave reader – and be amazed. You'll be stunned at how many foul facts there are to flabbergast your friends and freak out your family. And amazed that science can be so squishy…

UGLY BUGS

Bugs are seriously squishy and not just when you step on them. Take bees – you might think that bees make us honey out of the goodness of their little hearts. But bees are brutal stingers and African bees are even worse – they can be killers!

The buzz about bees

1 I bet you'd rather not know – but in 1964 a young Zimbabwean boy was stung 2,243 times by bees. He tried to hide from them in a river but the brutal bees stung him until his head turned black with stings and swelled up like a football. Amazingly he lived.

2 A scientist tried to find out how dangerous African honeybees really are. He juggled a ball in front of their hive to see how many times the ball got stung. But the bad-tempered bees attacked the stupid scientist instead. He was stung 92 times in a few seconds and ran 800 metres to get away. Sadly nobody clocked his time – it could have been a new world record.

SORRY DO YOU MIND DOING IT AGAIN?

And then what about flies?

1 Blowflies enjoy eating rotting meat and animal droppings. They lay eggs on rotting meat and even do terrible things to your Sunday roast.

2 The common housefly has common table manners. It drops in for dinner unvited and sicks up over its food. And then it's been known to serve up a free selection of over 30 deadly diseases.

The horrible habits of filthy flies mean that you can't even be safe from ugly bugs in your own home. And thousands of bugs have already set up home in your home…

Bet you never knew!
Your home is swarming with tiny creatures – called dust mites. These bugs don't do any harm but we can breathe in their poo and this can trigger asthma attacks in some people that make breathing hard. And the really bad news is that dust mites poo 20 times a day (If they used toilet paper it would cost a fortune!)

Hold onto this book, sit down and take a deep breath. Ready now? I've got bad news … you know those disgusting mites? Well, they don't just live in your carpets. Thousands of mites frolic in your bed every night – what's more they drink your dribble and poo in your pillow! You can't see them without a microscope but they're there. Let's imagine a mite wrote letters to her friend on the carpet. OK, I know this is mite silly – I bet they use mobile phones these days…

To Cara Petmite,
The carpet.

The Pillow

Dear Cara,
Greetings from Pillowtown! It's comfy here and everything's fine. Trouble is a giant human insists on getting into bed with us every night and he snores! Mind you, the night life's great - there's 40,000 of us and I've got loads of mites. How's things with you?
Your mite,
Pilla Mite

HI!

← SOME OF MY MITES

Dear Cara,
As I was saying it's great - I've got the whole family with me including grandma and great grandma. Great-great-grandma's dead now but I see her mouldering body every time I go for a poo. And there's loads of food!

CHOMP!

Actually that's all down to the human I mentioned. The human lays on dead skin and grease and tasty dried dribble for us to eat. Is that generous or what? And the human even keeps us warm - so mustn't grumble!

Write soon!

DEAD SKIN

Pilla

8

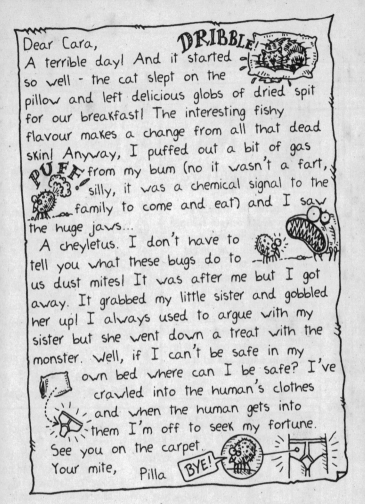

Dear Cara,

DRIBBLE!

A terrible day! And it started so well - the cat slept on the pillow and left delicious globs of dried spit for our breakfast! The interesting fishy flavour makes a change from all that dead skin! Anyway, I puffed out a bit of gas

PUFF!

from my bum (no it wasn't a fart, silly, it was a chemical signal to the family to come and eat) and I saw the huge jaws...

A cheyletus. I don't have to tell you what these bugs do to us dust mites! It was after me but I got away. It grabbed my little sister and gobbled her up! I always used to argue with my sister but she went down a treat with the monster. Well, if I can't be safe in my own bed where can I be safe? I've crawled into the human's clothes and when the human gets into them I'm off to seek my fortune. See you on the carpet.

Your mite, Pilla

BYE!

And now for the *really* squishy news. There are revolting mite relatives living in the tiny pits that your eyelashes grow from – now that is the pits. But elsewhere in the ugly bug world things are even squishier…

9

BEWARE IT'S A BOMBARDIER!

Get yourself the ultimate in personal self-defence systems! Beat off the bullies with a bombardier beetle gun. Unique self-mixing action for nasty boiling chemicals. Amazing internal heating system in abdomen heats chemicals to temperature of 100°C and fires at 500 to 1000 squirts a second!

The bombardier beetle gun is maintenance free. Just let it crunch on a few smaller insects now and then.

ELM BARK BEETLE TREE SURGEON

Unsightly elm trees getting you down? Need a bit more light? Call us now. Try our unique Dutch elm disease fungus formula – a revolting little rootless plant that terminates trees. We'll soon get in under the bark and wipe out the woody weeds!

▷ Forest felled.
▷ No job too large.

Disease established in UK - 1970s. Over 25 million elms eliminated.

BRIGHTEN UP YOUR HOME

With a firefly lantern. As used in Brazil, the West Indies and Far East Firefly lanterns cast a soft green or yellow light from the bodies of female fireflies. Forty fireflies are as bright as one candle. They need no power or batteries – it's all done with chemicals by your friendly firefly.

Sexton Beetle

and Sons and Daughters

Dead? Just call in your friendly family funeral directors. No job too large. We'll bury anything even if it means ten hour shifts. Free personal limb chopping service to make burials easier. Professional after-care service. Our little grubs will look after the grave. No fee charged but they do like to come to the funeral feast. That's to feast on the dead body of course!

NEED ANY DUNG SHIFTED?

Scarab Beetle Services will get rid of the lot. Dung ball rolling and burying our speciality. What's more we'll even lay our eggs on it and get our grubs to eat it!

'Scarab beetles were round before the dung hit the ground. They had 7,000 on the job and soon got rid of it all! My savannah has never looked tidier.' A.N.Elephant, Africa.

JEWELLERY WITH A MIND OF IT'S OWN

Ever wanted some jewellery that puts itself away at night? Buy some living jewel beetle jewellery as worn in many parts of the world. Choice of beautiful metallic colours including gold. Breaks the ice at parties, e.g. 'And what would your earring like to eat?' Manufacturer's warning: Don't allow your jewellery to lay eggs on your furniture. The grubs can lunch on your lounge suite for up to 47 years before turning into more jewel beetles.

Revolting recipes

Mind you, ugly bugs aren't all bad news – you can actually eat some of them – if you're brave enough. That's what millions of apparently sane people do throughout the world. Would you fancy a bug for breakfast?

Starters

Fried and salted termites

An African treat. Tastes like fried pork rind, peanuts and potato chips all mixed up!

L'escargots

Oui, mes amis! The traditional French delicacy. (Snails to you.) Fed on lettuce. Boiled and cooked with garlic, butter, shallots, salt, pepper and lemon juice. Served with parsley. Bon appetit!

Fried witchetty grub

A native Australian delicacy – these are giant wood-moth grubs. They look a bit like fusilli pasta and swell up when fried. Delicious!

Main courses

Stir-fried silkworm pupae

This tasty traditional Chinese dish is prepared with garlic, ginger, pepper and soy sauce. Wonderful warm nutty custard flavour. You spit out the shells. Very good for high blood pressure.

Roast longhorn timber beetle

Deliciously crunchy balsawood flavour. As cooked by the native people of South America.

Fried Moroccan grasshopper

Boiled bug bodies prepared with pepper, salt and chopped parsley then fried in batter with a little vinegar. You can also eat them raw.

Blue-legged tarantula

A popular spider dish in Laos in South-east Asia. Freshly toasted and served with salt or chillies. Flavour similar to the marrow in chicken bones.

Most bugs aren't eaten by humans – they're eaten by other bugs, such as spiders. So are you scared of spiders? Well, one scientist who wasn't was Allan Blair. In 1933 he let a deadly black widow spider bite him … as an experiment! Here's how the spider might have told her story…

13

So what happened to him?

ERK!

Well, the finger turned blue and red and then swelled up like a giant purple sausage. It was all very colourful. (And the things he was saying sounded even more colourful. But I'm a spider and I don't understand that kind of language!)

I heard the scientist went to hospital.

BZZZ!

Is it true the scientist was planning to let you bite him again?

BZZZ!

Yes, he was a bit wimpy if you ask me. All that stuff about sweating and vomiting and going mad with pain! He should be grateful he wasn't a fly!

Well, that was the idea – but he changed his mind for some reason. Never mind, sounds like there's something else for me to get my fangs into...

GULP!

STAYING FOR DINNER, AIREY?

So would you let a deadly spider bite you for science homework? Well, even if you're up for that – the creatures in the next chapter will give you goosebumps. They're REALLY awful!

AWFUL ANIMALS

Animals are awful. Awfully dangerous and sometimes awfully cruel. No wonder skunks fight back by spraying smelly juice. Here's how they warn other creatures to back off before it's too late…

SKUNK DEFENCE MANUAL

To be carried by all skunks at all times. You never know when you might need it.

1. Always give your attacker a warning. It's only fair to perform this little dance. Try practising it now.

◀ Stamp your feet and arch your back.

▶ Sway your body backwards and forwards.

◀ Stand on your hands and walk on them towards the attacker until you're about 2.5 metres (9 feet) away.

2. If they don't get the message, they're asking for it. Turn your back on the enemy. Raise your tail in the air. Arch your back. Look over your shoulder and check your aim. Ready, steady, FIRE!

3. You're sending a spray that comes from glands on either side of your bottom. Waggle your behind from side-to-side so your enemy gets a good drenching.

Personally, I'd back off fast – skunk juice is the WORST SMELL IN THE WORLD. If it gets in your eyes you can't see for a while, if it gets on your skin you'll throw up and if it gets on your clothes people will sniff you a mile off. And the only known cure is to take a bath in tomato ketchup. Mind you, compared to other creatures that's not too bad – at least skunks don't *poison* you…

Frightening frogs and toads

1 Frogs and toads have poison in their skin.

2 Some frogs go a little over the top in this area. The poison-arrow frog of Columbia, South America, is so dreadfully deadly that just 0.0001 g of its poison can kill.

3 And that means that (help … where's my calculator?) a yoghurt pot full of poison (weighing 28.3 g) could kill 2.5 million people! That's some frog.

4 In the 1970s scientists discovered the South American terrible frog. The poison from this frog is so deadly that the scientists had to wear rubber gloves to touch it. When a chicken and a dog touched the gloves they died.

5 If frogs are frightening, toads can be terrifying. A dog that chews a toad will throw up and foam at the mouth. It could die.

WHAT'S HAPPENED TO REX?

HE ATE A TOAD AND CROAKED.

But the real painful poison experts are snakes. (In fact I could write a book about horrible snake bites.) Humans have come up with some equally horrible and far less effective treatments…

YE OLDE SNAKE-BITE REMEDIES

1 Drink 4.5 litres (1 gallon) of whisky.

2 Cut off your snake-bitten finger with a large knife. Or you could shoot it off with your trusty six-gun. (Traditional cowboy remedy.)

3 Cut the wound open and ask a very good friend to suck out the poison.

4 Soak the bitten hand in paraffin.

5 Wrap chicken meat around the bite. Then burn the meat.

6 Eat a live snake.

7 Squash a toad and squeeze its juices over the wound. (Ancient Roman remedy)

8 Before you get bitten chew some of the snake's poison glands. Or you could make a small wound in your skin and rub in a mixture of spit and poison glands.

There's one creature that makes your average poisonous snake seem cute and cuddly. I'm talking about a giant monitor lizard from Indonesia called a komodo dragon. These loathsome lizards with bad breath enjoy munching the odd tourist (and what's more they munch tourists who aren't odd at all).

Mind you, the dragons are even crueller to each other – just imagine what a dragon's problem page would be like…

THE DAILY DRAGON
problem page…

Hi!

Are you a dragon in difficulties? Why not drop a line to your favourite animal agony aunt, Daphne Dragon?

Dear Daphne
I'm a baby komodo dragon with a terrible problem. My parents have bad breath and they want to kill me. What should I do?

Little Nipper

Dear Little Nipper
Your problem is perfectly normal. All komodo dragons want to eat their babies once they leave their nest. As for the bad breath — it's healthy for us dragons to have loads of germs in our mouths. They get into any creature

we bite and kill them. And we sniff out their rotting bodies (that's why no dragon should ever use mouthwash).

PS If you really don't want to be eaten try hiding in a tree or rolling in poo. The disgusting stink will put your parents off eating you. It worked for me!

Dear Daphne

I've never eaten with other dragons before and I've heard we can eat each other. Are there any table manners I should remember?

Hungry Snapper

Dear Hungry Snapper

Table manners?! You must be choking, er joking! Simply start with the guts, eat fast and don't be fussy. I'm especially fond of an over-ripe deer with a side order of maggots. If you don't like the maggots you can lick them off the meat and if they crawl up your nose you can sneeze them out! Bon appetit!

Of course not every creature makes a living out of killing other creatures. Some of them are quite helpful…

CREATURE COMFORTS SERVICES DIRECTORY

HEY FISH – D'YOU FANCY A WASH AND BRUSH UP?

Let your friendly cleaner Wrasse do the job for you. We'll nibble that nasty mould and fungus away and leave your scales as good as new! Speedy personal attention assured.

ALMOST FINISHED

"Cleaner Wrasse managed to serve a queue of 300 fish in a single session. Highly recommended."

A. Shark (Pacific Ocean)

WARNING!
To all customers of Cleaner Wrasse Services: BEWARE OF CHEAP IMITATIONS! Blenny fish try to copy Cleaner Wrasse. They've even copied the stripe on our bodies. But BEWARE! As soon as they get close they'll take a bite out of you and scarper!

You may have met one of the fiercest animal hunters already. Indeed this ferocious beast could be lurking behind your curtains or even watching your TV. Yes, I'm talking about your not-so-cuddly cat…

Tiddles has her own hunting territory. Normally she won't allow any other cat into this area. The territory is a little larger than your garden.

Tiddles hunts by sneaking up on prey. Sometimes she freezes before moving stealthily forward once more. At the last moment she pounces.

Tiddles enjoys catching insects. They have such a lovely crunchy texture – it's just like you eating crisps. But she doesn't like catching rabbits or rats. She's scared of rabbits because they're so big. And she thinks that rats taste worse than cheap cat food.

When Tiddles "plays" with mice she's not being cruel. Oh no? She's just a big scaredy-cat. Scared the mouse will fight back (some mice do). So she keeps her distance without losing the mouse.

Tiddles eats mice head first. Gulp. Before eating birds she plucks out the feathers with her teeth.

When Tiddles brings you a half-dead mouse or battered bird it's her way of teaching you to hunt. Yes – she wants you to finish it off. Mother cats do this to train their kittens.

Bet you never knew!

1 The champion hunter of all time was a cat named Towser. By the time she died in 1987 she had caught 28,899 mice at the Glenturret Whisky Distillery, Scotland.

2 A cat's skill in hunting once saved a man's life. The man in question was Sir Henry Wyatt, a 15th-century English knight who was locked in a dungeon and left to starve. But hungry Henry was befriended by a stray cat. The cat brought in birds such as pigeons and kept the knight alive until he was released by friends.

Have you ever wanted to chat with your cat? Well now you can – courtesy of Horrible Science! You see, animals recognize certain gestures and respond to them. We'll start with a crash course in ape language and move on to dogs and cats later…

1 Kissing gesture:
Meaning: Help me please, I'm a friend.
Note: If a monkey makes this gesture it's a good idea to copy it. Hopefully you won't actually have to kiss the monkey.

2 Smacking lips:
Meaning: I love you and I want to eat the bits of dead skin and ticks in your hair.
Note: Monkeys do this to their friends. So if you smack lips to a monkey you better be serious about it.

3 Teeth chattering:
Meaning: HELP! I'm scared!
Note: Does anyone else have this effect on you?

Dare you find out for yourself . . . how to "talk" to your pet dog/cat?
If you don't happen to have a pet monkey, you may look out for these expressions on a pet dog or cat.

1 EXCITED EYES   Blinking eyes = I'm upset

2 FEARFUL FROWN

Frown. (Eyebrows lowered and eyes half-closed) = There's danger ahead

3 A CROSS CREATURE

Eyebrows down but eyes wide open = I don't like you. Note: It's always extremely rude to stare at a cat or dog. They get upset and if they happen to be much larger than you they might decide to take a chunk out of you.

4 EAGER EARS

Sideways ears = I'm resting

Twitching ears = I'm about to pounce.

And now for a pet you probably *wouldn't* want to talk to. In fact you may not want it for a pet at all…

Bet you never knew!
In the 1990s a Hungarian couple bought a cute white puppy. They became a bit worried when their pet grew very big and smashed up their home. And they were even more alarmed to discover their puppy was really a polar bear!

GRRR!

ER… WALKIES?

Polar bears prowl the streets of Churchill in Canada. Believe it or not, a polar bear once even walked into a local club. The manager told the blundering bear it wasn't a member, so it walked out again. At Halloween local children aren't allowed to dress as ghosts because they might be mistaken for polar bears and shot with a knock-out dart.

Whilst we're talking about bears I can't resist telling you that scientists have discovered that one type of bear – the giant panda actually pees upside-down. Pandas pee against trees to mark their territory and by peeing upside down they impress passing pandas by leaving a higher mark. DON'T try this at home – toilet handstands can result in unfortunate accidents! But you're too smart to try – aren't you?

In fact, I bet you're so smart you'll get this squishy question right away…

Could you be a scientist?

You are working in a British oceanarium in 2001 and you've got a poison problem. Dottie the dicefish is feeling tense and squirting poison. How do you calm her down?

a) Play her a selection of relaxing music.

b) Give her a big toy dice to make friends with.

c) Stun her with an electric shock – BEWARE, you could be DICE-ing with death!

Answer: If you said c) be warned – it's extremely dangerous. And putting electrodes in your goldfish's bowl is a criminal offence! The answer is b)! Dottie was given a dice and, true to her name, daft Dottie decided the dice was her dad (or mum). Soon Dottie and her dice were deeply devoted. Would you make a mistake like this?

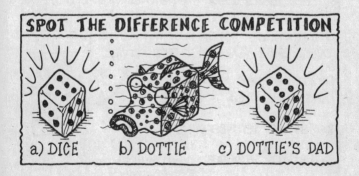

SPOT THE DIFFERENCE COMPETITION

a) DICE   b) DOTTIE   c) DOTTIE'S DAD

It's great being alive isn't it? Not only is it much more exciting than being dead – it also means that you can enjoy the workings of your seriously squishy human body…

LOOKING FOR A NEW BODY?

WHY NOT CHOOSE THE REAL MCCOY – THE ONE AND ONLY **HUMAN BODY**

IT'S PLANET EARTH'S MOST ADVANCED LIVING MACHINE! It's built of the finest materials to a tried and tested design that's over *two hundred thousand* years old! With a bit of care and attention your human body will provide over EIGHTY YEARS of superb service!

IT'S TRUE!

During this time your top-of-the-range human body is designed to…

▷ Talk for ten years. YAK! YAK!

OLD MAN

▷ Eat for 3.5 years. MUNCH!

▷ Take MILLIONS of steps and cover 22,500 km (14,000 miles). (The body can walk 19,000 steps every day without its feet falling off.) WALK!

28

FLEX! ▷ Bend and straighten its fingers 25 million times without needing new knuckles.

PUMP! ▷ Beat its heart blood-pump over 2.5 billion times non-stop at an average 73 beats a minute, 105,120 beats a day. (Every 24 hours the heart pumps 8,000 to 16,000 litres of blood and never goes pop!)

THINK! ▷ Store ONE MILLION bits of data in its brain memory - everything from science facts to shopping lists, plus your friends' birthdays, 100,000 words, all the players in your favourite team - and it can recognize over 2,000 faces!

~THE SMALL PRINT~
Remember, the body is designed to do these things over its lifetime. Body owners shouldn't expect their bodies to do them all non-stop!

The human body comes in two main body models - the MALE and the FEMALE, and both body models are available in a lovely choice of colours!

available in: light brown, dark brown, pink, beige and yellow

WOMAN   GIRL   BOY   MAN

THE HUMAN BODY - BET YOU CAN'T LIVE WITHOUT IT!

The amazing
BIRTHDAY SUIT

UNIQUE SAFETY PHOTOCHROMIC COLOURS

GET ONE FREE WITH EVERY NEWBORN BABY!

NO FADING

1. Your BIRTHDAY SUIT comes in a variety of colours all provided by its unique melanin pigments.

2. Ordinary clothes fade in the sunshine but your BIRTHDAY SUIT comes with a guaranteed darkening action under sunlight to protect the wearer from harmful rays. It actually creates extra melanin for this all-important purpose.

FRONT

CHOICE OF COLOURS

AUTOMATIC COOLING MECHANISM

3. This unique feature springs into action if the suit gets too hot. The water-cooling pipes produce sweat to cool the outside of the BIRTHDAY SUIT.

4. Every BIRTHDAY SUIT is guaranteed to contain about three million of these tiny water-cooling pipes (known as sweat glands) and each one is so tightly coiled that if you pulled it out it would be over a metre long! The total length of your pipe system is 3660km (2269 miles)!

MANUFACTURER'S WARNING

5. The automatic cooling systems can easily lose 1.7 litres (quarter of a gallon) of sweat every hour in hot weather, so make sure it's well supplied with water.

6. The sweat under the arms and between the legs contains chemicals that germs like to eat. Yum! The germs make the stale sweat all yucky and smelly. (Please see Care and maintenance instruction 9 – for everybody's sake.)

7. Some people use deodorants to tackle the little problem above. These work by blocking the holes in the cooling systems. Fortunately they don't stop most of the sweat from escaping otherwise the BIRTHDAY SUIT would overheat.

SELF-REPAIRING MECHANISM

AUTOMATIC COOLING SYSTEM

BACK

LOW MAINTENANCE

HARMFUL RAY PROTECTION

CARE & MAINTENANCE INSTRUCTIONS

8. Your BIRTHDAY SUIT needs very little maintenance because of its unique self-repair mechanism. If it gets torn or damaged it will simply re-grow!

9. All you need to do is to gently wash the outer layer in soap and water to remove any dirt and flaky bits. Don't worry if bits drop off – the BIRTHDAY SUIT will always grow some more underneath!

But just because your body is amazing doesn't mean it doesn't need washing and brushing. If you don't do this your amazing body will get worryingly whiffy.

Bodies behaving badly

Everybody gets bad breath but teenagers are the most scared of it – especially when they're off to meet boy or girlfriends. It's not surprising really – the average human spends two weeks of their life in lip-puckering sloppy snogging!

Meanwhile microbes breed in unwashed socks and cause cheesy feet. One traditional cure involved stuffing bran in socks to soak up the sweat. It didn't work but at least you could make it into a tasty breakfast cereal.

START YOUR DAY ON THE RIGHT FOOTING!

CHEESY BRAN

Curious case study: A low-down dirty crook

In 2000, a robber held up a bank in San Diego, USA. It seems everyone held their noses rather than sticking their hands up because the man was so smelly! Hmm, he sounds more like a "rank" robber! Police helicopters blared loudspeaker warnings about the smelly man. Soon afterwards, a nosy motel receptionist noticed a nasty niff from a new guest. She called the cops. A good detective follows his nose and that's just what the cops did – the man was soon arrested and "scent" to jail. He should have taken a bath – he'd have made a clean getaway!

Everybody needs food to keep their body going – but you have to be careful how you handle food. Germs can get into your guts on your food with sickening results...

How NOT to handle food

Here are some sure-fire ways to give germs a helping hand into your food...

- Sneezing into food.

- Coughing into food. This shoots germs from your mouth and nose into the air. Use a handkerchief. Do not wrap your food in the handkerchief or use it as a bandage afterwards. Germs can also get into your body through unwashed wounds.
- Handling food without washing your hands. (There are usually a few germs hanging around on your hands.)
- Picking your nose or biting nails. This is a marvellous way to pick up a few million germs. It's especially anti-social if you try to do both at the same time.
- Picking bits of food from your teeth with your fingers and then eating it. Not recommended.

Once you've safely swallowed your food it goes on…

A gruesome guts tour

Here's a gruesomely thrilling alternative to the usual boring tourist trip. Just imagine being shrunk down to the size of a pinhead and boarding a coach the size of a pea. Then imagine going on a guided tour of someone else's guts! And guess what? Your dinner's thrown in! That's if you feel like eating any . . .

The Horrible Holiday Company proudly present…

THE GRUESOME GUTS GETAWAY!

EMBARK ON THE TRIP OF A LUNCHTIME.

THE SMALL PRINT
1. If you get digested and turned into a chemical soup it's not our fault - OK?
2. There will be no toilet stops until the end of the tour.

1.00 pm Enter the mouth. Fasten your safety belts and close the windows securely. It's wet outside and we're about to dive down the gullet waterfall. Splosh!

34

1.01 pm
Amazing 9 to 13-second free-fall as we're squeezed 25cm (10 inches) down the gullet!

1.02-6 pm Five hour stopover in the stomach. Plenty of time to admire the slimy stomach walls with their 35 million digestive juice-producing pits.

▶ Enjoy the beautiful sunset effect as a red hot pepper makes the stomach glow.

▶ Listen to the mighty roar of the rumbling stomach as trapped gases squelch around amongst the food.

▶ Experience the gut-churning thrill of the stomach big dipper as it churns and churns again every 20 seconds. (If you feel a bit queasy, sick-bags are provided.)

6.00 pm A sudden lurch takes us from the stomach into the intestine. Then what better than a relaxing 6m (6.5 yards) cruise down the scenic small intestine? (Speed 2.5cm (1 inch) per minute.)

► Feel the lovely smooth gliding motion as we're squeezed along. The slimy gut walls help to stop the guts from digesting themselves.

► Marvel at the velvety insides of the intestines made up of five million tiny projections called villi.

► Gasp as we are covered in enzyme-rich digestive juices squirting down from the pancreas and liver.

► Wonder as the food chemicals are sucked into the villi.

► Puzzle over the mystery of the appendix. Everyone's got one of these finger-like things sticking out of their intestines. But no-one knows what it's for!

10.00 pm Spend the night in the comfortable and spacious large intestines. Here the surroundings are peaceful, lie back and listen for the relaxing gurgling of the water as it's taken out of the remains of the food and back into the body.

7.30 am (Give or take a few hours). Put on your life jacket and parachute. It's time for splash down in the toilet!

But things can still go badly wrong…

A sickening story

You're dizzy, you turn pale, you sweat and your mouth is full of spit. You're about to chuck up. Run for the bathroom! The muscles in your lower body and stomach all squeeze together until your half-digested food erupts from your gullet. Vomiting, as it's called, is controlled by a part of your brain known as the vomiting centre. It's well-known that throwing up can be triggered by fear. Scientists don't quite know how this happens. They think that your nerves produce chemicals that make your stomach heave when you're scared of something.

What your vomit looks like depends on how long it's been in your stomach. If it's only been there for a few seconds it won't look too different from when you ate it. Especially if it happens to be carrot stew. But if it's been down for a couple of hours it will be a thick soupy mess. Scientists call this disgusting substance chyme (pronounced chime). How chyming, er, sorry, charming.

Meanwhile at the other end of the guts your body gets rid of all the waste food it doesn't want. But if you're stressed or don't eat enough roughage (stuff like bran that helps your guts keep your food moving) you get constipated. It's an uncomfortable subject.

Curious case study: It's tough on the throne

King Ferdinand I of Naples (1751–1825) had chronic constipation. When the straining sovereign found the going tough, he invited a crowd of friends into the Royal toilet to keep him company. The Austrian Emperor Joseph (1741–1790) was one of them:

WE MADE CONVERSATION FOR MORE THAN HALF AN HOUR AND I BELIEVE HE WOULD STILL BE THERE IF A TERRIBLE STINK HAD NOT CONVINCED US THAT ALL WAS OVER.

Toilets can be dangerous places. One night in 1856 Matthew Gladman went to the loo in his home-town of Lewes, England. Unfortunately the toilet floor had been removed prior to cleaning the pit underneath.

PLOP!

GENTS GENTS

BLIMEY, THAT WAS A BIG ONE!

Matthew fell into a deep pit of doo-doo… Gladman wasn't a glad man! He suffocated from the gruesome gases made by the rotting poo in the loo. And talking about gruesome gases…

Five facts that you always wanted to know about farting but were afraid to ask!

1 As you've just found out, kings fart. Presidents fart and so do Emperors. Children fart and even teachers are said to make the odd trouser cough. The only difference is how much, how often and how loudly they let it out.

2 One early account of farting was by ancient Greek playwright Aristophanes (about 448–380 BC) who makes a character in one of his plays say, "My wind exploded like a thunderclap." Sounds nasty.

3 Farting is your body's way of getting rid of air that you've swallowed by eating fast, talking whilst eating or swallowing bubbly spit. The more you burp the less you fart. Better not try explaining this important principle at family meal-times.

WHIFF

FARTY SMELL

PONG

IT'S YOUR FAULT MUM - YOU DON'T LIKE ME BURPING!

4 US astronauts are banned from eating foods, such as beans, before a space-flight. Well, would you fancy being cooped up in a cramped spacecraft on a ten-day space mission with an idiot who has bottom problems? You can't even open a window if things get too smelly!

5 Did you know that farting killed one man? Simon Tup was a Victorian entertainer – well, it's entertainment if you like that sort of thing. His act known as "the farting blacksmith" actually involved farting in time to music. Sadly, one night Simon's version of "Blow high and blow low" proved too much. He let out a huge fart and burst a blood vessel and died. It must have been a dreadful blow...

Simon died before he could see a doctor, but in his day a doctor might have helped him to die even faster! Those old-time docs were even more deadly than the diseases they were trying to cure…

How does a germ like a virus manage to spread through your school and make friends with all your friends? It's a seriously squishy question…

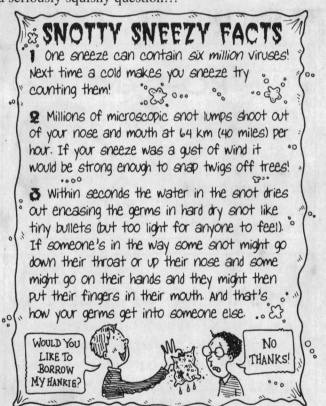

SNOTTY SNEEZY FACTS

1 One sneeze can contain six million viruses! Next time a cold makes you sneeze try counting them!

2 Millions of microscopic snot lumps shoot out of your nose and mouth at 64 km (40 miles) per hour. If your sneeze was a gust of wind it would be strong enough to snap twigs off trees!

3 Within seconds the water in the snot dries out encasing the germs in hard dry snot like tiny bullets (but too light for anyone to feel). If someone's in the way some snot might go down their throat or up their nose and some might go on their hands and they might then put their fingers in their mouth. And that's how your germs get into someone else.

WOULD YOU LIKE TO BORROW MY HANKIE?

NO THANKS!

Up to the 1900s most of the treatments your doctor could give you were useless – or worse than useless. And some were even worse than worse than useless. Here are a few terrible treatments from ancient Egypt…

Horrible Healthcare presents...
ANCIENT EGYPTIAN CURES YOU'LL BE DYING TO TRY!

Try new RO-DENTURE!

Split open a mouse and lay its warm body along your gums. You're sure to squeak through – even if the mouse doesn't!

SSSLUB!

Try new GARLIC GARGLE

– now with EXTRA garlic! It's guaranteed to tackle terrible toothache. And it's sure to get rid of sore throats AND unwanted visitors! Try it on your dog and his bark will be worse than his bite!

UGH!

Is this "toe" good to be true? Accidents will happen, but if you find yourself short of a few toes, don't despair! Egyptian doctors have invented...

THE WOODY-TIDDLER WOODEN BIG TOE

Lovely choice of woods and colours!

"My toenails look great with wood varnish and they never need cutting!" Satisfied patient.

Tired of weeping wounds? Cure your cuts with new

MILKY PLOPS!

POOEY

PONG!

Milky Plops contain the finest high-quality poo and full-cream milk. You plop them on your wounds and they'll heal in a flush, er, flash.

It's a sight for sore eyes! If your eyes have cloudy areas (cataracts), why not try

BRAINY-BALM?

It's made from genuine chopped-up tortoise brains mixed with honey.

SMEAR IT ON YOUR EYEBALLS MORNING AND NIGHT TO PUT YOUR SIGHT RIGHT.

Dreadful dentures

Of course if your toothache got too bad and the old dead mouse didn't work you could always have all your teeth pulled out and replaced with false ones. Nowadays false teeth are made from tough plastic but in the past people had to make do with really disgusting dentures…

SAMPLE THE JOYS OF SPRING!

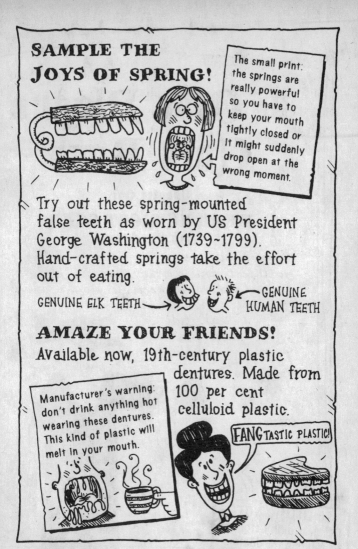

The small print: the springs are really powerful so you have to keep your mouth tightly closed or it might suddenly drop open at the wrong moment.

Try out these spring-mounted false teeth as worn by US President George Washington (1739~1799). Hand-crafted springs take the effort out of eating.

GENUINE ELK TEETH →

← GENUINE HUMAN TEETH

AMAZE YOUR FRIENDS!

Available now, 19th-century plastic dentures. Made from 100 per cent celluloid plastic.

Manufacturer's warning: don't drink anything hot wearing these dentures. This kind of plastic will melt in your mouth.

FANGTASTIC PLASTIC!

From time to time outbreaks of killer diseases such as the plague or black death would sweep the world and kill millions of people. And – you guessed it – most treatments were useless!

Ye Olde Plague Cure Book

Chapter One

WEAR YE RIGHT GEAR
(1348 version)

Doctors all over Europe are wearing ye latest anti-plague gear. Ye high-tech clobber will keep ye plague away!

Beak full of nice smelling herbs

Mask

Wand for checking a victim's pulse

Long leather gloves

Leather gown

SCIENTIFIC NOTE
This gear didn't stop the fleas biting the doctor and causing plague.

Chapter Two

A BREATH OF FRESH AIR

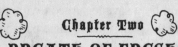

As everyone knows, ye plague be caused by some kind of nasty smell in ye air. So it helps if you...

Light ye bonfires or set off ye cannon. Smoke gets rid of ye smell. Smoking tobacco is _good_ for ye because it gets rid of smells. Everyone should smoke including ye children.

HISTORICAL NOTE: Cannons and tobacco were seventeenth century, the others were 1348. Children were beaten by their teacher at Eton College, England, for *not* smoking.

WHACK!

BUT SMOKING IS **BAD** FOR YOU!

To get ye air moving in a healthy way try letting birds fly round ye room or ringing a few bells.

DING! DONG!

If ye don't have ye gunpowder or ye birds or ye bells ye needs to fart into ye bottle and uncork it to let out ye odour. Ye whiff will chase out ye foul air that causeth plague (and ye friends too). If ye have not ye bottle why not simply stick ye head down ye blocked toilet?

YE FARTY PONG!

If you got injured, things became even squishier. You could be operated on by a savage surgeon without even a headache pill to dull the pain. One in three patients died.

Some patients tried to escape. A patient of surgeon Robert Liston (1794–1847) ran off and hid in the toilet. The surgeon chased the patient, broke down the toilet door and carried him back to the operating theatre. He lived.

Mind you, Liston wasn't always so successful. Can you believe it – he actually did an op on one man that killed THREE men! Here's how it might have sounded on the radio (if they had had radios in those days).

Welcome to Top of the Ops Live. My name's Mike Commentator and we're here to witness history being made. Today surgeon Robert Liston will be trying to break his own world cutting-off-the-leg speed record of 150 seconds...

And here comes Liston now. He's dressed in his usual blood-spattered green coat and Wellington boots. He's looking calm and relaxed — which is more than I can say for the patient!

Liston's calling for his assistant to time him. He's drawing his knife — it's got a notch in the handle for each of his previous ops. And he's off. He's cutting into the leg. The patient is struggling and screaming. He's being held

down as Liston slices around. the bone OH MY GOODNESS! Liston's cut off three of his assistant's fingers. The knife must have slipped — it must have been all that blood. And it's sliced off a piece of patient too! Liston's pulled out the knife and — OH NO I don't believe it! He's cut the coat-tails off a spectator. The man's fainted — NO, HE'S DEAD! He's had a heart attack because he thought he'd been stabbed.

And now the operating theatre is in chaos! The blood is squirting everywhere, the patient is screaming, the assistant is screaming — I'm SCREAMING!

But Liston is sawing the bone and tying up the blood vessels as if nothing has happened. What a performer! But I'm sorry to say that Robert Liston has failed to break his world cutting-off-the-leg record. And now he's got to do it all another day! I guess he'll be looking for another patient to practise on!

NOT OVER MY DEAD BODY!

OR MINE!

OR MINE!

The patient and the assistant were killed by germs. But even when surgeons invented germ-free ops in the 1900s some docs tried their hands at useless surgery. American Walter Freeman (1895–1972) invented a revolting and quite pointless brain op for mentally ill people…

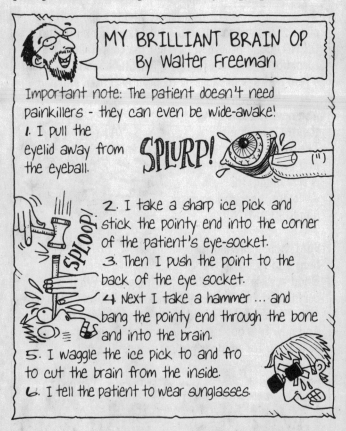

MY BRILLIANT BRAIN OP
By Walter Freeman

Important note: The patient doesn't need painkillers - they can even be wide-awake!

1. I pull the eyelid away from the eyeball. SPLURP!

2. I take a sharp ice pick and stick the pointy end into the corner of the patient's eye-socket.

3. Then I push the point to the back of the eye socket.

4. Next I take a hammer … and bang the pointy end through the bone and into the brain.

5. I waggle the ice pick to and fro to cut the brain from the inside.

6. I tell the patient to wear sunglasses.

Well, I suppose the patient did see the "point" of the ice-pick but the op destroyed their personality and did no good. SO DON'T TRY THIS AT HOME!

KILLER CHEMICALS

And talking about things you shouldn't do at home – you really don't want to mess with the chemicals in this chapter. They're killer chemicals and look what they did to these poor people…

POISON MURDER CASE FILE

VICTIM'S NAME: Agathocles
JOB: King of Syracuse
DATE: 289 BC
PLACE: Sicily
POISONED BY: His grandson
HOW POISONED: He was using the pointy tip of a feather to clean bits of food from between his teeth. But the king's wicked grandson had dipped the feather in poison. The poison stopped the king from moving (it might have been a type of nerve poison). Everyone thought the king was dead so he was given a traditional ancient Greek funeral. His body was burned – but he was still alive!

POISON MURDER CASE FILE

VICTIM'S NAME: Bianca Capello
JOB: Poisoner
DATE: Sixteenth century
PLACE: Florence, Italy
POISONED BY: Herself
HOW POISONED: She was trying to poison Cardinal Ferdinand with a rather tempting poisoned tart. But the clever cardinal switched the sweets and Bianca bumped herself off by mistake.

POISON MURDER CASE FILE

VICTIM'S NAME: Michael Malloy

JOB: Tramp

DATE: 1933

PLACE: New York

POISONED BY: Bar owner Tony Marino, his barman Daniel "Red" Murphy and undertaker Frankie Pasqua.

HOW POISONED: Tony and Frankie were down on their luck. Tony's bar wasn't making too much money and Frankie's funeral business was dying on its feet. So they decided to poison the homeless tramp and claim a big insurance payout. Trouble was the tramp didn't die. They gave him...

● Antifreeze to drink. Malloy glugged it down and asked for more. DON'T TRY THIS AT HOME! Antifreeze is deadly even in small doses.

● Rotten sardine sandwiches and rotten oysters. Malloy asked for seconds.

At last, after failed attempts to run Malloy down and freeze him to death, the gang gassed the tramp with carbon monoxide. But the cops were hearing bad stories about Tony Marino and the boys. So they dug up Malloy's body and its pink colour proved how he'd died. The corpse might have been in the pink but the gang looked a lot less healthy when they were executed the following year.

Two more painful poisons

Lead is dangerous. Sixteenth-century ladies used white lead face powder to improve their complexions. After a few years the poison ruined their skin – it absorbed the lead and gave them blood poisoning. But the ladies didn't know why their skin was ruined so they used extra lead to cover up the damage!

One of the nastiest killer chemicals of all time was a substance called arsenic. Many years ago it was used to make fly papers. Flies stuck to the paper and came to a sticky end as the arsenic got to work.

Unfortunately a few humans went the same way too. Arsenic has no taste and no smell and that made it ideal for painful murder poisons.

Murderous metal weapons

1. The first iron weapons were made from meteorites that fell from outer space.

2. In 1500BC people worked out how to heat iron-ore to make metal, but it wasn't very strong.

3. Iron needed to be mixed with another metal before it was really strong. In 1200BC people first added carbon to iron to make it stronger.

> ONE PORTION OF CARBON

4. Meanwhile soldiers fought with bronze swords. But they often bent in battle!

HA HA HA

5. Iron swords were much harder, sharper . . . and more deadly.

SWOOSH

And that wasn't all. There followed iron guns and iron cannon firing iron cannon balls. This led to more chaos on the battlefield and buckets of blood being spilt. And oddly enough, there's iron in blood too.

Some poisonous metals can have dramatic effects on their victims.

Thallium for example makes the skin too sensitive to be touched. The victim can't smile or change the expression on their face. They lose control of their eyeballs and their hair drops out.

Mercury is even worse. It builds up slowly in the body damaging the brain and kidneys and causing madness. The victim can't pee easily and they end up with yellow skin, black gums and no teeth.

And even when they weren't used to kill people on purpose, some chemicals could be deadly, as these Poison Products ads prove…

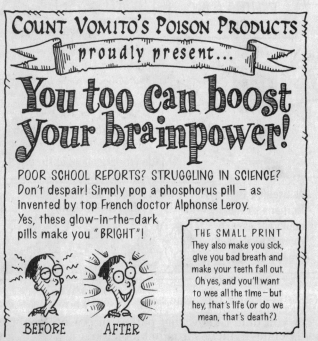

COUNT VOMITO'S POISON PRODUCTS
proudly present...

You too can boost your brainpower!

POOR SCHOOL REPORTS? STRUGGLING IN SCIENCE?
Don't despair! Simply pop a phosphorus pill — as invented by top French doctor Alphonse Leroy.
Yes, these glow-in-the-dark pills make you "BRIGHT"!

THE SMALL PRINT
They also make you sick, give you bad breath and make your teeth fall out. Oh yes, and you'll want to wee all the time — but hey, that's life (or do we mean, that's death?).

BEFORE   AFTER

Animals can be poisonous. OK, so you know that – but I bet you didn't know that pufferfish poison has been used to turn people into zombies! That's the view of scientists who claim the poison may have been used on the island of Haiti. Would you want to turn your brother or sister into a zombie? Thought so! Well, here's how the scientists think it was done…

THE DIY ZOMBIE KIT

NOW YOU CAN TURN YOUR BROTHER OR SISTER INTO A ZOMBIE SLAVE IN THE COMFORT OF YOUR OWN HOME!

All you need is…
A BROTHER OR SISTER

Our special top-secret zombie poison mix, which includes real genuine baby bones and pufferfish poison.

All you do is…

Give your brother or sister some poison (not too much now — you don't want to really kill them!)

DON'T WORRY, IT'S DELICIOUS!

With the right dose, your victim appears dead and gets buried. Then, all you have to do is dig them up and put them to work tidying your room and doing your science homework!

PROMISE YOU'LL TIDY MY ROOM – CROSS YOUR HEART AND HOPE TO DIE?

So there's NO WAY you'll be trying this at home? Well, I'm glad to hear that because it saves me the bother of telling you that there may be a law against poisoning members of your family and using them as slaves. And anyway most scientists aren't too sure that the zombie poison recipe was genuine.

Appalling acids

One all-too-genuine group of chemicals are the acids. In the right place they can be quite helpful – lemon juice is an example. But in the wrong place acids are appalling. Take acid rain for example. Industry and traffic make sulphur-dioxide gas, which makes rain more acid. Acid rain eats away at buildings old and new – even your school is in danger. Oh well, every acid rain cloud has a silver lining!

Acid rain doesn't dissolve people – thank goodness – but funnily enough it can turn blond hair green. The awful acid reacts with copper in water pipes to form copper sulphate, which causes the interesting colour change.

But acid rain can be more fatal for other living things. It kills trees by the million…

And it does terrible things to fish. They don't grow and the acid dissolves their bones.

Squishy sulphuric acid

Talking about dissolving bones – the final killer chemical in this chapter is a stronger acid. Sulphuric acid is oily and colourless and turns things to sludge – including your body if it spills on you.

It does have its uses, of course – you can use it to make fertilizers or see-through paper and so it's often added to toilet paper. Luckily the acid is washed off to avoid appalling injuries to your backside. But these aren't the only things the acid has been used for…

In 1949 businessman John Haigh was charged with murder. He had disposed of his victim's body in an appallingly horrible way by dumping it in sulphuric acid. Haigh had boasted to police that there would be nothing left. As he said at the time:

HOW CAN YOU PROVE MURDER IF THERE'S NO BODY?

But Haigh was wrong. The acid had not destroyed the evidence. There were a few grisly tell-tale bits remaining – and a complete set of plastic false teeth. These were promptly identified by the dentist of the murdered woman.

I'D RECOGNIZE THAT GRIN ANYWHERE

Haigh then admitted getting rid of five more bodies using the same method. He went on trial at Lewes Assizes. The jury took 18 minutes to reach their verdict and John Haigh was executed.

FATAL PHYSICS

Physics is the branch of science that includes forces and energy and space. And because this book features the horrible bits of Horrible Science we'll take a lingering look at the most squishy areas of physics – the fatal bits!

Gruesome gravity

A force is a power that makes an object move or at least squashes it – so if an elephant drags you out of bed on a Monday morning then its using a force. Let's hope it doesn't squash you instead. The best-known and most gruesome force is gravity.

In the past gravity was used to make executions more efficient. During a hanging the victim dropped through a trapdoor and gravity acting on the rope broke the victim's neck. If the drop was too far the force yanked their head off too. Gruesome!

I DON'T FEEL WELL

YOU'LL FEEL REALLY ROPY IN A MINUTE

Another gruesome method of execution was the guillotine. This featured a 30.4 kg weight attached to a sharp blade. The force powering the gruesome blade as it fell was gravity. In the 1790s working model guillotines were popular children's toys. Their parents must have been off their heads.

POOR TEDDY!

In England in the seventeenth century criminals who refused to plead guilty or not guilty at their trials were crushed to death under heavy weights. Once again it was gravity doing the damage. You may be interested to know that a louse can withstand a force of 500,000 times its own weight. Unfortunately for the criminals, humans scrunch more easily.

YOU ROTTEN LOUSE!

IF ONLY I WAS

One of the squishiest effects of gravity is jumping from a plane … and forgetting your parachute. Even with a parachute, it's a terrifying experience – but that didn't stop US scientist Harry Armstrong making notes on how he felt … you'll be pleased to know he lived to tell the tale!

MY PARACHUTE JUMP
BY HARRY ARMSTRONG

So here I am in the plane. I feel a mixture of fear and excitement - well, fear mostly. I really should have gone to the toilet when I had the chance. Oddly enough, I'm so scared that I can't hear the plane's engine. It is still working, isn't it? I'm trembling with nerves - please forgive the shaky writing.

TREMBLE!

OK, this is it - I'm at 670 metres. I'm about to jump … wish me luck!

ARRRGGGGGGGGGGH!
I'm tumbling head over heels at 190 Km per hour (please forgive the even more shaky handwriting). I think I'd better close my eyes. Oh — that feels oddly relaxing — I think I'll Keep them closed … Hmm — but what if I hit the ground before I open my eyes? YIKES! I could even wake up to find myself dead! Hmm, I'd best open my eyes. I'm at 579 metres and the ground is coming up to meet me. Er, hello, ground! Now where's my parachute rip cord? Oh no, that's my shoelace …

TUG!

Trouble in store

Harry couldn't have made his jump without an energy store. Your body manages to keep going between meals by storing energy in the form of fat, Harry's plane had fuel as an energy store. But there are lots of other ways to store energy – as this accident-prone teacher is about to show us…

THE ADVENTURES OF PUT-UPON PHIL

This rock has potential energy – that's stored energy for the future so it can...

WOBBLE!

...FALL DOWN!

The elastic rope stores movement energy as it stretches.

STRETCH!

BUNGEE JUMP

OOPS!

SNAP!

The spring inside this cannon stores energy.

 BOING!

Where's the safety net?!

Now I have lots of potential energy...

 The way this bomb stores energy is fascinating...

TICK-TOCK!

The spring in this clock stores energy from winding.

And the dynamite stores chemical energy... of course it's quite safe ...

BOOM!

THAT'S IT — I QUIT!

When fuel catches fire the effects can be even more fatal and squishy. Of course any old scientist knows that fire is really a chemical reaction in which fuel combines with oxygen gas from the air to give out its stored energy in the form of heat and light. But that doesn't make it any less PAINFUL…

Fatal fiery facts…

1 Burning alive was the punishment in many countries for opposing the Church or being a witch. If the executioner felt kind they might smear the victim's body with a kind of fast-burning tar called pitch to finish them off faster.

FANCY SOME PITCH?

TAR VERY MUCH!

2 In England women were burnt alive if they killed their husbands or clipped bits of silver off coins. The last woman to suffer this fate was Christian Murphy in 1789. A witness said:

She behaved with great decency, but was most shocked at the dreadful punishment she was about to undergo.

No wonder she was shocked – if she'd been a man she'd have got off with a nice quick hanging.

3 Burning wasn't the only method in which fire helped to get rid of people. In ancient China criminals were fried in oil. The English King Henry VIII (1490–1547) ordered that people found guilty of poisoning should be boiled alive.

4 Archaeologists have studied skeletons from Herculaneum, a Roman town destroyed by a volcano in AD 79. The people had been killed by superheated gases and the archaeologists found that their brains had boiled whilst they were *still alive*.

5 Some people are said to burst into flames for no obvious reason – this is known as spontaneous human combustion. One possibility is that farts contain gases such as phosphane (fos-fane) and methane that catch fire easily. So perhaps the fires are caused by fiery farting? Oh well, what a way to glow!

Killer cold

If there's one thing worse than too much heat it's too little. Cold is just as fatal as heat. As the body cools the brain shuts down with fatal results. And extreme cold switches off the blood supply to your fingers and toes. Eventually they die and drop off – a condition known as "frost-bite".

Bet you never knew!

1 Frostbite was a killer condition for early explorers who were trying to reach the North and South Poles. One day American Robert Peary (1856-1920) took off his boots and eight of his toes fell off. He later remarked:

A FEW TOES WERE NOT MUCH TO GIVE TO ACHIEVE THE POLE

Do you agree?

2 In 2000 a museum received an unusual donation. Major Michael Lane sent them five of his own fingers and eight of his toes. They had been lost to frostbite when he was climbing Mount Everest in 1976.

"I don't think it was quite what they were expecting," remarked the gallant mountaineer.

3 In 1991 frostbite claimed both the hands of heroic Korean climber Kim Hong Bin on Mount McKinley, USA – but he made it to the top using his legs and teeth.

SCARY OUTER SPACE

Even the coldest parts of Earth are warm and cosy compared to outer space – space is colder than minus 100°C – cold enough to freeze your skin solid. But if you've forgotten to put on your spacesuit getting frozen is the least of your worries…

Let's see what happens when an alien suffers the fatal effects of being in space without protection… (Yes – I know that scientists say there's no proof that aliens exist – this is a made-up story!) The aliens decide to go for a spacewalk…

ARE WE READY?

YOU BET! I COULD DO WITH SOME FRESH AIR!

YOU'VE FORGOTTEN YOUR SPACESUIT!

Although space is bitterly cold, sunlight can be hotter than 120°C – that's hot enough to burn skin to a crisp. So the alien is frozen on one side and roasted on the other!

With no air to press on the alien's body, the air inside her pushes out and she swells up like a balloon. Soon her guts and lungs and eyeballs are about to explode.

And without the force of the air pressing on her body all her blood and body juices start to boil like slimy cabbage soup.

Meanwhile deadly rays from the sun zap the alien and cook her from the inside like a turkey in a microwave. But just when she's about to die she's rescued by her alien pals and repaired in the spacecraft's sick bay. Well, that really is lucky – any human who tried this would have been killed!

Mind you, there are even squishier ways to get killed in space. You could go too close to a giant exploding star, or a nasty neutron star or a black hole… Well, to be honest, our rockets aren't powerful enough to get there just now but just imagine that you could…

Sinister superstar secrets

Big stars are bad news. I'm talking about a star bigger than our fairly well-behaved star known as the Sun. Big stars guzzle up their supply of hydrogen gas (the stuff stars are made from) in about 11 million years and blow up.

The Big Bash bursts the star to bits in a blast brighter than ONE BILLION stars! It's called a supernova and it's a real super-star show-stopper. And that, you might think, is that. But it's not. The big star shrinks to the size of a large city. But it doesn't die – it turns into a scary mini-monster called a neutron star. Would you fancy a neutron-star holiday?

Horrible Holidays present...

The Neutron Star Hotel

Check into our out-of-this-world ONE-STAR hotel...

WELCOME!

GASP!

Unique atmosphere! It's so heavy that it's only 2.5 cm high. At least you can enjoy an all-day lie-in as you struggle to breathe!

Work-out in our exclusive gym. Just lifting your head uses more energy than climbing Mount Everest.

URRRRRGH!

You'll want to come back as soon as possible. And even if you don't – the gravity will pull you back!

Here's some facts that the Horrible Holidays people should have told you before you made your booking… The neutron star has GIGANTIC gravity. Even a tiny flake of snot on your hankie weighs about a million tonnes and that's why you can't escape. Oh well, at least it's scientifically fascinating.

Some neutron stars are known as pulsars. They spin so fast that the whole star can turn 360° in less than a second. And they blast out beams of radio waves like whirling flashing space sirens.

But there is one type of neutron star that makes that seem rather relaxing. I'm talking about the mean, murderous magnetar.

The magnetar is like a giant magnet – but you wouldn't want one on your fridge. If a magnetar was where the moon is, its force would rip away every bit of magnetic metal on Earth and wipe clean your dad's classic music cassette collection. And that's the nice bit…

The fearsome force would turn all the humans on Earth into slime soup by re-arranging every bit of matter in their bodies. And that really is no laughing matter!

But, for really big stars – those weighing more than 20 Suns – an even more frightening future is in store. Something that makes the magnetar look warm and fluffy. With these really big stars, the bit left after the supernova blast shrinks into … A HORRIBLE BLACK HOLE! Visiting a black hole could spoil your "hole" day – but if you wanna try it…

Horrible Holidays present...

The Black Hole Hotel

Why not "drop-in" for a "hole" lot of fun?! It's more than just a hole, it's a hole in the universe. And you'll find its pull hard to resist! Once inside, you'll enjoy a quick break! Well, several breaks, as your body is pulled into long stringy bits and squished smaller than a pinhead and never seen again...
You'll be thrilled to bits...

YES, VERY LITTLE BITS!

Sounds seriously squishy to me. But not quite as squishy as the facts in our next chapter…

Horrible Science is full of squishy bits – but that raises a horrible question. What's the squishiest bit of all? What's the foulest fact in science? Well, I guess that's a matter of opinion but here are a few of my favourites.

Physics facts are fantastically *foul*…

Airship pioneers suffered a fearsome fiery fate when their airships blew up. In 1897 German Karl Wolfert was cooked in his craft and his burnt body fell on a crowd of bigwigs who had come to see his test flight.

In 1901 Brazilian August Severo suffered the same fate in Paris. A man and his wife were snoring in their bed when two bloody, broken bodies landed on their duvet.

In 1878 inventor Thomas Edison (1847–1931) wanted to invent anti-gravity underwear that floated around in mid-air! A drawing of the time shows a dad towing his floating children.

But wait, would YOU fancy turning up at school in a pair of ground-defying knickers?

Killer chemical facts really do *stink*…
In Denmark in 2000 a gang of girls sneaked into a toilet to sniff butane gas. These girls had the brain power of an absent-minded woodlouse. Butane is a poisonous gas used for cooking, so it burns easily. Guess what happened when one of the girls lit a cigarette?

Well, what do you expect? Smoking is BAD for you! And the girls were smoking non-stop after they caught fire. Taking poison is stupid and those girls were playing with fire.

In 1996 an Italian club owner was found guilty of pumping laughing gas into his club. Maybe he was trying to make people laugh at his jokes, but the judge didn't see the funny side. The crazy club owner was fined. What's that? You fancy playing a trick like that too? OK, go ahead, just so long as you don't mind losing all your pocket money for the next 2,000 years.

The science of animals is *naturally* squishy…

In June 1996 a Chinese hunter named Li from Shanxi Province was feeling bored. He came across a snake and thought it might be fun to prod it with his gun. The surprised snake coiled around the gun, pulled the trigger and blasted Li in the bum. He died soon afterwards … shot by a snake!

In 2003 scientists in Canada found that fish send messages by farting bubbles. Herring keep in touch at night using high-pitched bottom burps. No one knows if sharks have musical bottoms but you're welcome to find out … if you dare!

In 2002 a hippo-attack victim arrived in hospital in Zululand, South Africa. His whole face had been bitten off and all that was left was one eyeball. Incredibly, the patient doctors called "the miracle man" survived the attack.

Medicine is *sickeningly* squishy…

In 1995 a man went into a Florida hospital to have his leg amputated. "You're sure you know which one you're going to cut?" he joked to staff. The anaesthetic knocked him out and surgeons cut off the wrong leg.

When an epidemic struck the cities of ancient Turkey an ugly person was chosen to be sacrificed to the gods. They ate a barley loaf, dried figs and cheese, and they were beaten with fig branches. Afterwards, the chosen person was burnt alive and their ashes scattered in the sea. Oddly enough, this practice didn't stop the epidemic and no, your teacher wouldn't have been the victim so stop daydreaming and read on...

In Jamaica in 1740 Dr John Williams announced yellow fever was different to blackwater fever. This is a fever (surprise, surprise) in which your pee turns brown or red (but not usually black). Local doctor Parker Bennett disagreed and challenged Williams to a duel. In the fight both doctors were killed.

THE M★ST SQUISHY FACT ... EVER!

So which of these facts is the most squishy? The answer is NONE of them!

I think there's one fact that's even more revolting, even more squishy than any in this book so far. Ready to hear it? Here goes…

Remember the last time you used the toilet? I bet you thought the revolting contents of the toilet vanished around the bend. And they did – mostly… But a cloud of droplets flew up and covered you in water and not just water, pee and tiny lumps of poo from the toilet! You can't see the droplets without a microscope – but they really were there. But DON'T PANIC – you've been flushing the loo for years and never come to any harm!

One thing's for sure – there's more to science than boring boffins. Science belongs to us all – it's the most amazing way to discover the universe and everything in it. And if science can be serious – it's also seriously funny, seriously exciting and seriously squishy. But you'll know all about the squishy bits already!

Happy Horrible Science everyone!

Science with the squishy bits left in!

Ugly Bugs ● Blood, Bones and Body Bits ● Nasty Nature
Chemical Chaos ● Fatal Forces ● Sounds Dreadful ● Evolve or Die
Vicious Veg ● Disgusting Digestion ● Bulging Brains
Frightening Light ● Shocking Electricity ● Deadly Diseases
Microscopic Monsters ● Killer Energy ● The Body Owner's Handbook
The Terrible Truth About Time ● Space, Stars and Slimy Aliens
Painful Poison ● The Fearsome Fight For Flight ● Angry Animals
Measly Medicine

Specials
Suffering Scientists ● Explosive Experiments
The Awfully Big Quiz Book ● Really Rotten Experiments

Two horrible books in one
Ugly Bugs and Nasty Nature
Blood, Bones and Body Bits and Chemical Chaos
Frightening Light and Sounds Dreadful
Bulging Brains and Disgusting Digestion
Microscopic Monsters and Deadly Diseases
Killer Energy and Shocking Electricity

Large—format colour hardback
The Stunning Science of Everything
Dangerous Dinosaurs Jigsaw Book